D1073336

Home with Henry

Home with Henry
A Memoir

Anne Kaier

Illustrations by
Carol Chu

PS BOOKS
Regional Publishing, National Voice
A division of Philadelphia Stories

Published by PS Books, a division of Philadelphia Stories, Inc.
ISBN 978-0-9904715-1-6

Cover Image: © 2014 Carol Chu
Cover Design: Sarah Eldridge
Book Design: Sarah Eldridge

PS Books
93 Old York Road
Ste. 1-753
Jenkintown, PA 19046

www.psbookspublishing.org

For Ed

March

Monday, March 17, 1997

Driving home from work tonight, I saw a small orange cat lying stunned on the blacktop in the middle of my lane. Slowing down, I loosened my green velour scarf and leaned forward on the steering wheel to get a better view. The cat's ears still pointed up and its tail seemed to thrash, but I knew it was only a matter of time before an impatient driver felt the cat's back crackle. Cat pizza. Horns began to bark behind me. Swedesford Road's always jammed around 5:30 with all those bloody commuters. I edged forward. The overhanging trees flicked across my sightlines. The kitty lay low to the ground. Surely, if I kept the wheels straight, my car's undercarriage would skim over the mass of fur. Clutching the wheel, I kept a steady two miles an hour until my back tires had moved safely past. In the rear view mirror, I saw that the cat still lay, undisturbed, on the asphalt. It seemed OK. I figured maybe I'd done enough. At least I hadn't killed it. Picking up speed so the commuters behind me wouldn't go crazy with their honking, I drove away from the cat, passing four or five houses. I had had a long day at work—editing copy for the new brochure the sales reps have been bugging me for. Home and a glass of wine sounded great. How many dead cats did I see beside the road? I couldn't stop for every one. But in my mind's eye, this little creature still sprawled in the middle of the street, its bright orange fur a temptation for huge tires. I had to go back.

I pulled my dear old Ford Escort off the road, slammed the car door, and walked up the middle of the cat's lane, raising my hand to stop an oncoming blue pickup and the stream of cars behind it. The guy in the blue truck seemed surprised that a middle-aged woman in a gray coat would hold up traffic, but I enjoyed that momentary feeling of power. I glimpsed the orange fur and reckoned the cat was probably dead by now, with flies whirring around its mouth and nostrils. But when I picked up the limp creature, it felt warm in my hands. Walking back to my car, I held it against my chest and it shat a little on my green scarf. I put it on the passenger seat and covered it with an old beach towel as you are supposed to do with people in shock. I edged back around the car and wedged my ever-widening hips into the driver's seat. Now what?

Dr. Royster's vet clinic, about twenty minutes away, would still be open. He once told me a story about Chops, the stray cat whose jaw he had stitched together after a car tire had snapped it in a traffic accident. Dr. Royster would know what to do. "Hold on, kitty," I said. As I drove, I stroked the cat's left ear, saying, "There, there, kitty." I didn't know how hurt it was. Didn't know whether it was male or female. But the blond fur in the cleft behind its ear felt almost downy.

In the vet's back parking lot, I slid into a compact slot near Dr. Royster's red sports car. Leaving the little creature on my passenger seat, I walked into the clinic, breathed its smell of powerful cleanser, and told a vet tech that an injured cat lay stock-still in my car. For fear of aggravating its hurt, I told her, I didn't want to lift it myself. Would she help me, please? The assistant knew exactly how to carry the numb animal. She brought it in and put it on a metal examining table. The cat immediately sprang off and scooted to a corner of the room, trying desperately to hide. The assistant wisely kept her distance. When I told Dr. Royster what had happened, he said, "Well, he's a stunned and very scared tomcat." Then, almost casually, he leaned over and picked him up. Clinging like a towel to Dr. Royster's generous shoulder, the cat gradually stopped flailing. "I'll get him started on an IV," the vet said, "and we'll see how he is tomorrow."

I started to wonder how much this was going to cost me. I hate sudden shocks to the budget, especially when I don't have any idea how much the bill might be. But the die was cast. I couldn't desert the little cat now. Perhaps because I knew Dr. Royster would be unlikely to find a new home for yet another unwanted animal. Perhaps because I'd felt the warmth behind his ear. Perhaps because I couldn't bear the image of myself closing off my heart and walking away. A few weeks before, I'd been driving home from work when another cat who'd been hit in the left lane had caught my eye. I'd circled around, stopped my car, and walked over to it, but the black cat lay with fixed eyes, lifeless on the tarmac. I'd lifted it up and laid it in the grass by the side of the road, not wanting its body to be mangled by oncoming cars. Clearly, something was going on in me, some willingness to let myself be disturbed. I had room somehow, emotional room, for something new.

Out in the vet's green waiting area, the assistant got ready to make a new entry in her computer log. "Did you find any tags on him?" she asked, clicking away. "Probably not, eh?"

"Ah, no."

"OK. We'll just call him ..." She stared at the screen. "Your other cat's Lucille, right? Twelve-year-old ..."

"A calico, yep."

"OK, we'll just call him Stray Cat Kaier."

I balked at this. "No, he's not just a stray. He's a tomcat."

"Right," she muttered. "A stray tomcat."

"Call him Tom Kaier, for the moment, until I can think of something else." She looked quizzically at me. I smiled and tilted my head. "My nephew's called Tom Kaier," I said. "Just turned ten."

"Ah."

"Don't think he'd be too pleased to share his name with a cat."

That was for sure. Tommy has a sturdy sense of his own self-worth, judging by the number of presents he got for his birthday last week, his favorite being particularly blood-thirsty monster games on some kind of little computer thingy you hold in your hand. I knew the cat needed a better name. But I left thinking if we called him a stray, he'd stay a stray. Something in me rebelled against thinking of him like that. I'd rescued him. I needed to protect him, get him in under a roof somewhere. I didn't want any creature I'd rescued to be homeless, to just wander around—perhaps because I'd wandered about too often in my own adult life, moving into a different apartment almost every two years from the time I came back to Philly after graduate school until I finally bought a house at age fifty, little more than a year ago. Walking out to my car, I shook off the vision of Tom Cat Kaier shivering under a tree, alone in the suburban woods. Somewhere, I determined, he would have a home.

Tuesday, March 18

When I called the vet from my kitchen at seven o'clock this morning, he said the little guy wasn't doing so well—wasn't moving around in his cage. I felt an immediate letdown, but Dr. Royster hadn't finished. "We'll keep up the medicines and see if he responds," he said. Then he paused. "Are you really serious about keeping this cat?" Perhaps we were both thinking about how expensive those medicines were. It might not make sense to continue treating him if he didn't have a good home on the horizon. How old was he? I asked. How much of his life would he have left if he made it through the next few days? Almost all of it, Dr. Royster told me, a note of hopefulness in his voice. He figured the cat was barely a year old. Maybe that decided me. I honestly didn't know what I'd do in the end, but I knew I couldn't abandon him.

"If he survives," I told Dr. Royster, "I'll take him—or find someone who will."

When I'd hung up the phone, I veered into the living room, rubbing my forehead. For a few moments, I stared out the big windows. My neighbors' cherry tree looked like a mauve smudge against their stucco this morning. Sitting on the green sofa, I twitched my legs. Why on earth had I agreed to take in a feral cat? It's not as though I go up and down the block feeding strays. Lucille's the only cat who's ever lived with me.

Two fire engines yowled out on Pine Street. Every siren from every bloody ambulance or cop car in the city of Philadelphia still scrapes my ears. I can't get used to them or tune them out. They disturb the peace.

Lucille came by and rubbed against my leg, never noticing the plaques of heavy dry skin on my shins. "This psoriasis-type thing doesn't worry you, does it, Miss?" I said. Patting her flank, I wondered how she would manage  with a wild, male cat around. When I bought this place fourteen months ago, she came with me—my only companion. How the living room, with its bare chestnut floors, echoed! What was I thinking, moving into my first house at age fifty with one cat? For the first few weeks, I'd felt terrified. I was downright crazy, my friends said. I'd hear strange hums in the house. One night I even imagined that guys were working on the gas lines that snake around under the Victorian brick houses and brownstones in our neighborhood. I convinced myself that the drilling let gas escape in little bursts. That, I thought, accounted for the hums I'd been hearing, so I went out into the street to investigate. A Philly cop on a big black horse came clopping by. I went up to him and asked about the gas guys working on the infrastructure. He looked at me as if I were a little nuts. "No, ma'am, nobody's working underground around here." The news was discouraging because it meant I had no way to account for the hum in my ears, which persisted for a while. I realized later that it probably came from grinding my teeth because I was scared to be alone in my house. Still I had Lucille. She loved to run up and down the stairs. She hadn't been able to do that in my condo—or in my apartment before that, even though she liked to sit on the windowsills and look out at the birds. But stairs come with a town house. One room per floor, just about, one on top of the other. Three floors in all. A city house. Great for Lucille. I can't imagine the place without her. But, of course, I can imagine it without her. Without any cat, any living creature. Maybe that's what underlies this picking up cats in the road business. I'm downright terrified to be alone. What if I lost Lucille?

Thursday, March 20

The little cat is better. Dr. Royster called to say he'd seen the tom circling his cage, clicking his nails against the metal. He hasn't sustained any serious injury. I guess the meds kicked in. We finally talked about money. "Since you're going to take him," Dr. R. said, "I'll only charge you the minimum for hospitalization and neutering." We had a deal.

On the way home tonight, I stopped to see my awkward kitty. He hunkered in the back of his cage, hissing and spitting. The vet tech spoke softly to him and Dr. Royster reassured me. "He's just scared," Dr. Royster said. "He'll come around." After a few minutes, the little guy quieted down, only growling now and then in a half-hearted way. Somehow I sensed his sweetness under all that bluster. I do that kind of thing, too, when I'm nervous or shy.

Driving home to the city, I considered what to call him. Since I picked him up on St. Patrick's Day, I thought Patrick might work. But he didn't seem cocky enough to be a Patrick. Maybe Patrick Henry, after the Revolutionary War hero. Still didn't seem right. My frightened cat wasn't exactly an eloquent orator. Finally, I settled on Henry. That seemed to fit—at least for the moment. I figured I'll have to see what he's like.

At home, I set up a kind of studio apartment for Henry in the guest bedroom on my third floor. A fresh-smelling litter box waited in a corner, yellow ceramic bowls sat ready for food and water. A clean Phillies sweatshirt huddled on the closet floor. For good measure, I tossed a beach towel into another corner. He'd have his choice of cozy places to sleep.

Monday, March 24

Henry came home today in a stiff cardboard carrier. He stayed quiet in the car, assessing the situation, but as I started up the stairs to the third floor guest room he began to jerk in short spurts inside his box. Would he scratch his way out before I got him safely into his room? I clutched the cardboard kennel with one arm while I unlocked the guestroom, hoping he wouldn't claw my elbow to bits. Closing the door behind me, I put the box on the floor and opened it slowly. He didn't move a muscle. He sat terrified, looking at me with enormous pupils—as if I would strike him. He had nowhere to go. No way to save himself. Murmuring soothing sounds, I tried to comfort him, but he was having none of it. Here he was, in a strange place in the city, far away from grass and trees, with a strange creature looming over him. Finally, he jumped out of the box, ran around the room at breakneck speed, and flung himself feet first against a casement window that overlooked my garden three stories below. The glass panes held during repeated assaults as he thrumped against them, but by now I felt terrified for him. I imagined him breaking through the window, falling past the stucco wall, and smashing on the garden pavers. My heart went out to him, but I didn't dare get too near for fear of scaring him even more. After a while, he gave up and hunched himself against a corner near the bed, looking up at me with his great green eyes. "It'll be OK, little fellow," I said. Backing away, I inched toward the door, slipped out, closed it, and went downstairs, giving him time to get used to his terrifying new home.

Tuesday, March 25

Henry's hiding under the guestroom bed. This morning, when I got down on my stomach and lifted up the cotton dust ruffle to look at him, he hissed and spat. His breath smelled foul. He kept his eyes on me, staring at me steadily. I inched the dust ruffle down and stayed there for a few minutes, breathing softly. It seemed like the right thing to do. Obviously, I don't know anything about taming a feral cat. And I can't seem to locate a good book on the subject—books being one of the primary ways I find out about the world. But it looks like Henry's found a safe hiding place and is determined to protect it.

He hasn't touched the closet nest I made for him with my sweatshirt, but some magazines that had been stacked on the floor in a corner of the room looked disheveled this morning—as if he had come out from under the bed at some dark hour and run around the room. Fresh paw marks spotted the casement window panes. Had he been flinging himself against them again?

The kibble I'd poured into his yellow bowl had disappeared, so I assume he ate it. What did he eat in the wild suburbs? Mice? Moles? His coat shimmers; it's clean and thick. Maybe he sheltered in a barn. A few farm families still hold onto their arable acres, now woven among corporate buildings out in the Great Valley where he tomcatted around. Maybe Henry lived on a spread like Dunkins Farm—the place I take my spicy nephew Tommy Kaier for pumpkins in the fall. Tommy always picks an odd-shaped pumpkin. He has an eye for the unusual, our Tommy.

But the farms have mainly given way to new con-
struction—long lines of stiff houses rising like toy
soldiers on treeless grids. I remember when I first went
house hunting, a realtor took me to one of these new
tracts. I was about to turn fifty and I guess I'd finally
convinced myself that if I were ever going to have a
house of my own, which I deeply wanted, I'd have to
ignore the fact that I wasn't married and wasn't likely to
be married any time soon, wasn't even dating anyone interesting. If I wanted a house, I'd have to go out and find
one. This realtor drove me around in a spotless Lexus
to see affordable "townhomes" in new complexes near
our office. They all looked like crackerjack houses, and I
was sure a wolf would blow them down if he huffed and
puffed enough. One good hurricane would certainly do
it. The last place she took me was a "gated community."
No one is allowed in without checking with a guard at
the security hut out front, and the complex is completely
walled. I loathed the place on sight, but she didn't get the
hint. Tossing her glossy blond hairdo and turning toward
me, she smiled knowingly. "You're a single working gal,"
she said—did she actually say "gal"? "You belong in a gated community." That was probably my moment of truth.
I knew perfectly well I did not belong in a gated community. I hate places that exclude other people, closing
their doors to the swirl of ordinary life. For that matter,
limits of any kind make me thrash about. I wasn't going
to be locked up somewhere or stuck in anyone's designa-
tion for a single woman. If a gated community or a crackerjack house were the only places an unmarried person
could live in the suburbs, I decided to forget living in the

suburbs—despite the trees and grass and crickets I loved. To hell with the 'burbs and their gates and happy families. I'd go live in the city where interesting single people live. In a house. Someplace lovely and unusual with, hopefully, a garden. I'd have to give up my dream of living in deep country, way out in open farmland where, I imagined, I would feel a profound peacefulness in the natural world. But if I could find a real garden with my city house, I could bring something of the country's bloom into the city. Back at the realtor's parking lot, I swung my purple paisley skirt out of the Lexus and never called her again.

Wednesday, March 26

Lucille licked a caramel-colored spot on her back this morning and then ran upstairs with me to help check on Henry. She lay quietly on the other side of the closed door while he and I visited. I didn't dare let her meet him yet. It's as if she's the big sister being coaxed into accepting the newcomer. At least I can touch Lucille and give her kisses and pats.

About half the kibble still rattled around in Henry's yellow bowl. Maybe he wasn't hungry last night, though with all this stress and chasing magazines across the floor when I'm not there, you'd think he'd be starving. Maybe he's missing his moles and his mice. When I got down on my stomach and elbows, lifted up the dust ruffle very slowly and said hi to the little guy, he hissed and spat in a desultory kind of way, as if he were just going through the motions. Probably his cat mom taught him to carry on like that whenever some intruder poked into his hiding place. I sang softly to him for a few minutes, holding the dust ruffle up with my right hand. After a while, he began to turn his head away, as if he felt he didn't need to keep his eyes on me at all times. He tucked one front paw underneath his chest. Was it a sign of cold (it was cold in the room)—or a sign of relaxation? The very fact that he could ignore me seemed like progress.

Friday, March 28

Meanwhile, Miss Lucille doesn't seem one bit perturbed. Last night, she lay outside the door to Henry's room and meowed to come in. I wouldn't let her, but she didn't hiss or kick up a real fuss.

Today I lay in bed late and listened to her rustling around under my box springs. When she hopped up next to me, I stretched my left arm out and she tapped it with her paw before throwing the weight of her flank against it. How warm she felt, how deeply her warmth seeped into my arm. We lay peacefully for a while until I had to rouse myself so I'd get to work on time. Sitting on the edge of my bed, I scratched her soft, fat tummy. "What shall I wear today, Lucille?" She pawed the air, then turned over, got up, shook herself, and sat next to me, quite unconcerned with my fashion choices. I rubbed her ear and stood up. "You have beautiful whiskers at all times," I said, moving slowly into the bathroom, "a perfect adornment." A few minutes later, she nosed her way in and sat looking at me while I reached my hands around my back to clasp my bra. "And you never have to get into a bra," I said, "because you have all that lovely fur to cover your titties." She had tucked her paws under her and sat looking directly at me. I ruffled the hair on her forehead. "Yet another reason why cats are superior to people. Is that what you think?" I picked out a chic red sweater, slipped it over my nicely rounded breasts, and went downstairs.

In the kitchen, she ate her plump tuna while I took my coffee into the garden. Morning light speckled

Lenten roses and fell across a pot of blue pansies. Their plush faces peered up from leaves bedraggled by the winter. Putting my coffee down on the white plastic table, I thought how lucky I'd been to find a city house with a real garden—though the hunt had taken a year. My Center City realtor, a thin Irish guy who didn't think it at all unusual for a single woman to want a house, found this one for me in a neighborhood where lots of single people live—judging from the number of them who walk through our pocket park on Friday nights to gather at the local pub. My realtor also understood that I sometimes need to walk barefoot out of my back door and listen to the chickadees calling. An old yew tree springs up in my garden, deciduous trees wave within my sightlines, and at this time of year I can feel spongy earth beneath my feet while I hunt for daffodil tips in my flower beds.

Looking around at the old stucco walls this morning, I rejoiced that my neighbors can't quite see me, though their whistles and laughs leap over the parapets—along with the keen of a buzz saw now and then. I leaned back in my chair, thinking this place would be nice for a couple, except that the men I've dated have all been smart, funny—and totally unmarriageable. Take David, my "English boyfriend." Red hair and freckles flocked on his forearms. We wandered around Oxford when I was in grad school, meandering past ancient college buildings, golden in the sunlight. David knew an enormous amount about classical music. He took me to hear Beethoven's Violin Concerto in the oldest concert hall in Europe. But he bent over me in a stooped, old-man sort of way though he couldn't have been more than thirty. I was

what? Twenty-three? He had a blue bedroom where gray
sheets crumpled round his pale legs. When he asked me
to marry him, he said, "I would, you know." As if he were
offering something other guys wouldn't. Not many did,
as it turned out. Still, I didn't see myself as a charity case.
But all the guys I like are quirky. I can't get interested in
solid citizens—and they're looking for someone prettier,
younger, and less independent than I.

A pigeon's cry shook me out of my thoughts. I hung
onto the sound for a moment and then elbowed the
coffee cup out of the way, knowing myself to be an
outspoken, fifty-year-old woman with a skin problem
like psoriasis who is reasonably kind and smart. Not easy
to find intelligent, tender guys who go for this package.
Sweeping my hand across the tabletop, I noticed scratch
marks in the plastic and vowed to make a tablecloth to
cover the ruts.

Lucille wandered out after her breakfast, sat for
a while on the brick patio next to a yellow rose bush,
and then decided to get herself nicely washed. First
she swept her right paw across her black ear and down
the brown side of her face. Then she licked the grunge
off her white sock with her bristly tongue. She took no
notice of me while she did this. When she had polished
the black side of her face, she started in briskly with
the white side and repeated the whole procedure until
she considered herself finished. Then she settled into
a sunny patch where ivy, slightly gray from the winter,
trailed onto brick pavers. She would have sat there, quite
content, for the rest of the morning, but after about
twenty minutes I had to finish getting dressed and leave

for work. I brought my coffee cup into the kitchen, then
went back out, cruised over to Lucille's spot, picked
her up by her warm flanks, and admired her long white
whiskers. I brought her inside, plopped her down, and
locked the garden door behind me. Maybe I can leave
that door open in the summer, at least for short peri-
ods when I'm home. I'm foolishly afraid she'll run away
and I'd lose my best companion—though even if she did
wiggle through the gate that connects my garden with the
neighbors' in the back, she still couldn't get to the street
except through their front door. There's no alley in this
old complex, as the realtor pointed out when he sold me
the place. Stucco walls and wooden gates separate my
garden on all three sides from my neighbors' leafy patios.
It's paradise for cats in my garden. Bushes to hide under.
A tall yew tree to climb. Walls to sit on so a cat can see
into the neighbors' greenery though the humans can't.
Quite a nice setup.

Monday, March 31

Today I went to Petco at lunchtime and stamped out Henry's metal nametag. God knows when or how I'll get this blue collar around his skinny neck. But if Henry's officially mine, he should have my phone number jangling on a pendant. When I got back to my office, I slipped across the hall to the graphics department where the art directors work. Glasses shoved up in her hair, Andy peered at her computer screen. Either she was contemplating font colors up close or eyeballing her layout. Andy's the sort of person who takes in hurt birds. She probably feeds a whole pride of stray cats on her property. She grew up on a farm in South Jersey and is an expert on wild creatures of all kinds. I snuggled down against the wall of her cubicle. There's barely enough room for her computer and a tiny desk.

"Why don't the books tell you how you tame a wild cat?" I asked.

She was Photoshopping our new sales brochure and didn't take her eyes off her work. "Those books about choosing the right kitten are beside the point," she said, clicking pixel by pixel. "Everybody gets hand-me-down cats."

I crossed my legs under my hippie skirt and fiddled with the beaded hem. "But how am I going to get Henry out from under the bed?"

"Maybe he doesn't want to."

"Doesn't want to what?"

"Come out." Andy has a very sane attitude toward these things—and she always takes the animal's side. I told her I was worried about how Lucille would adjust.

"Lucille should sympathize," she said, reaching across me for her French vanilla coffee. I ducked a little, hoping it wouldn't drip on my head. "She was a rescue cat, too."

"She's forgotten all that."

Andy finally looked at me and told me that no cat forgets being put out on a porch in a hurricane with her kittens as Lucille was, even if she did wind up in a happy home. I rubbed my thigh. "Thank God I didn't have to take the kittens," I said and told her how the guy who rescued those tiny firecrackers called them "the kittens from hell." He had to beg people to adopt them. I scratched my itchy back against the cloth wall of her cubicle. People in the hallway laughed and talked about opening day for the Phillies. "The first night I had Henry home," I said, "I tossed a towel in a corner to make him feel comfy. He peed on it."

"And why not?" said Andy. I told her I'd taken it down to the basement to wash it and Lucille smelled and smelled it and then looked at me with wide eyes. "She wants to know what's going on," said Andy, "and she wants to know what you are going to do about it."

"So do I," I muttered, getting up. "So do I."

Wednesday, April 2

That boy is a savage, undomesticated creature. Last night, thinking Henry might be less shy if he spent a stretch of time sensing my unthreatening presence in his room, I went upstairs to sleep in the guestroom bed. It's Henry's bed, to all intents and purposes, even though it's where Tommy sleeps when he comes to spend the night. Henry's warm butt stuck out from under the dust ruffle and I couldn't resist trying to pat him. Such a much of hissing and spitting ensued! He ran around in his kingdom under the bed and defended his turf. At least I know he can move on his haunches. He seems basically healthy. His coat looks full and fluffy. He doesn't look starved. In fact, he looks nicely rounded. Someone must have watched over him or else he was clever about feeding himself. Maybe a farmer fed him. I can see him eating Meow Mix in a big wooden barn like the one down the road from our office.

Up on the bed, I read my history of the Normandy landings for a while, cocking an ear for Miss Lucille, who meowed outside the door for a few minutes before padding off downstairs, doubtless to one of her comfortable spots. Henry didn't make another sound. I thought about the first night Tommy stayed with me in this house, about a year ago. He was nine. We did all the usual things—ordered a pizza, rented a movie, curled up on my green living room sofa to watch the show. Tommy sat jiggling his legs in an easy rhythm. When something exciting happened in *The Lion King*, he turned and looked directly at me, opening his eyes wide, mimicking the voice of the evil Scar who clearly didn't faze him. After an hour, I got up and walked a few steps toward the kitchen with the pizza box in my hand. Then I looked back at Tommy, who had shimmied down to the floor and lay on his stomach. When I turned toward the kitchen again, a wave of sadness came over me—so strong I could barely see. The room swayed around me through a kind of gray-blue filter. Dimly, I understood that I would never see children of my own in my house. For twenty years, I'd jumped from one apartment to another, figuring, as many women of my generation did, that I'd move into a house when I married—if I ever found the right guy. I'd finally stopped waiting, and now a beauty of a house surrounded me and wonderful kids came to visit, but they were borrowed. It was too late to have any of my own and I'd never had the courage to adopt a child and raise her by myself.

In the kitchen, I shook off my swoon. Opening the freezer, I pulled out some Ben and Jerry's Cherry Garcia. Ice cream. Why not? When I handed him his bowl, Tommy muttered, "Awesome." Then he flipped back over onto his stomach and said "shloop, shloop" before he dug in.

Thursday, April 3

Since I have no instructions to guide me—and since I'm too much of a technophobe to hunt up sites on the Internet thingy about introducing domestic cats to wild cats who have just moved in—I took matters into my own hands last night. Maybe I simply didn't have the patience to wait any longer to see how Henry and Lucille would get along. Anyway, I scooped her from the sofa and took her up to meet the new guy. They could at least be in the same room, if not eyeball to eyeball. She squirmed in my arms all the way up the stairs and growled a little as we sat on the floor next to his bed. She tapped my shoulder with her right paw and then she flicked her tail and pushed against my elbows. She wanted to get down and investigate but I grasped her tight. No body contact allowed. Behind his dust ruffle, Henry didn't make a sound. He had no intention of revealing his lair. Even though I'm sure she knew precisely where he hid, she didn't squirm out of my arms, so the semi-introduction went off without a hitch.

Friday, April 4

On the whole, Henry's been very good about using the litter box, "an important survival skill for a cat who just came indoors," as Dr. Royster remarked the other day. But last night Henry had a big stinking accident on the carpet, leaving two turds right beside his bed. Honestly, it wasn't his fault. I rushed around like a madman myself yesterday evening, trying to deal with the trash and get out to dinner on time. Here's how it happened:

At 7:14 p.m., I drove down Twenty-fourth Street, coming home from work. Friends were waiting for me at the corner pub. We'd agreed to meet at 7:15. But it was trash night, so I had to run in, get the trash, and put it out on the curb before I went to dinner. It shouldn't have been a problem, but a policeman on a big black horse sat solid as a statue a block away at Twenty-fifth and Pine. If he saw me double-parked, I'd get a ticket. I put my blinker lights on, ran inside, ripped open my mail, changed Lucille's litter, dashed upstairs, emptied all the litter out of Henry's box, stumbled downstairs, and took the trash out to the curb just as the sanitation truck was coming down Pine Street accompanied by the policeman on the horse, clip-clopping along the tarmac. I jumped back into my car, parked it in a legit spot, went to the pub, ate dinner, and came back home. Then I slammed around downstairs, opening every closet door and banging them closed—so sure was I, in my craziness, that burglars had snuck into the house in my absence. When I finally went upstairs, I found that, in my haste to get the trash out, I'd forgotten to put any fresh litter in Henry's box, so he just had to do his business on the carpet. Poor guy. This was made for Arm & Hammer.

Saturday, April 5

Maybe it's wishful thinking, but did Henry emit something like a purr last night when I walked into his room with a steaming hot piece of chicken? Andy says to have patience. I slowly lifted up the dust ruffle, cooed and spoke kindly, and gradually pushed the piece of chicken in front of him—about five inches from his face. His nose looked like a hot red point punctuating his white snout. He blinked at me, then he sniffed the chicken and got his paws ready to pounce. But he wasn't going to make his move while he could still smell me there. When I went back twenty minutes later, the chicken was gone and Henry lay with his paws tucked under his chest. I deduced that he either has an extremely conservative outlook on life and doesn't like to take chances on anything new—like coming out from under the bed while I'm there—or he is still scared.

This morning, I phoned Dr. Royster again. "He'll come around," he said. "All he needs is time, love, and attention." I asked him how Henry was going to get love and attention if he didn't come out. "It's such a different environment for him," Dr. Royster said. "The city, no grass, easy meals." I guess the only answer is time.

Lucille marched into the third-floor bedroom this afternoon as I lay on the floor talking to Henry. Needless to say, he stayed under the bed. I can leave the door open while I'm in his room. Since he's always snug in his lair, I don't worry about him running out of the room. Lucille made a loud meow when she crossed the threshold, as she often does. She's a very talkative cat. Maybe she has a trace of Siamese. Henry put his two front paws out like a sphinx, blinked his pretty eyes at me, and shifted his hind quarters, but he didn't make a sound. She sniffed around behind me for a minute. Then she turned and walked away. Maybe they should get acquainted without me in the room. No, not yet. I'm not quite sure what Henry might do to her. He's wild and has claws. If they got into a fight, could she defend herself with only her back claws? Oh, I so regret having had her front claws ripped out all those years ago. What was I thinking? Worrying about the silly furniture. My dry skin dots the slipcovers and I don't like it, but I put up with it. A couple of cat scratches won't ruin the sofa. And there's always lemon juice. A squirt or two will keep the cats off any chair you please. Well, I'll have to watch how they get along—if he ever comes out from under the bed.

Tuesday, April 8

My whole family came to dinner on Sunday. Like a nice bro, Edward made himself useful in the kitchen, pushing cloves into the ham and chopping up veggies for salad. He cut each carrot and each red pepper very precisely, like the good lawyer he is, so we ended up with perfectly diced orange and red bits in the lettuce. The older kids helped their dad for a few minutes. He's got Charlie thinking it's cool to be a sous-chef and wash the greens, though that may not last long after Charlie becomes a teenager in two weeks' time. But then, Charlie is such a sweetheart he probably won't change. Lucille wandered around, making herself pleasant, greeting the guests by sniffing their hands now and then, but she was old hat—even for Tommy, a confirmed feline aficionado. The real excitement sprang from "the new cat." They all wanted to see him—as if Henry would come down and show off like some beast on a catwalk. But although Tommy raised his eyebrows at the notion that the new kitty might have shared his name, he seemed willing to follow me up to the third floor to see if Henry could be seduced from his hiding place.

As we climbed the stairs, I had one of my double vision moments, watching myself watching Tommy, thinking of myself in the third person as a favored aunt going upstairs with her nephew. I'm never entirely sure of myself with the kids, as much as I love their quirky company. Did Tommy really want to visit my new cat? Or was he just humoring his aunt? I tripped a little on the sharp curve up to the landing. But Tommy scampered ahead. Light on his feet like most ten-year-olds, he stepped quietly into Henry's quarters. Needless to say, that furtive feline hid way under the double bed. Tommy got down on his hands and knees and kind of crooned for a while, trying to coax Henry out. Then he dangled Henry's new—unworn—blue collar in front of him. Children have a wonderful capacity for forgetting who else is in the room, and Tommy chatted with Henry for about five minutes in a pleasant, singsong voice just right for a cat. "You should come out and play, Henry," he said, jangling the collar on the rug in front of Henry's pointy nose. "Annie has a pretty collar for you." But Henry wasn't moving one muscle and Tommy finally gave up.

I tried to explain. "He's shy, honey. Like a wild creature, really."

Tommy got up off the floor, shaking his blond head. "He's kinda weird, Annie." God knows Henry isn't one bit like tame old Gem, the cat Tommy knows at home. Gem often dozes for hours in a vintage wooden cradle in the dining room.

"Never mind," I said. "You can come for a sleepover when school lets out. Maybe we'll have better luck then." I'm not sure Tommy was convinced that two months would make much difference in Henry's social skills. Neither was I, for that matter.

After we'd eaten and done the dishes and they'd all left, I went upstairs to talk things over with Henry. Lying on the floor with a pillow under my chest, I kicked off my red leather shoes and chatted at him for about twenty minutes. I admired the streaks of straw-colored fur on his forehead—as if a painter had added a few last strokes

of paler yellow to his face. After a while, he finally felt
relaxed enough to turn his head away from me, putting it
down on his front paws. He didn't think he had to keep
his eyes on me every minute. I saw this as a step forward.
He seemed so soft, so young—barely a year old. Henry
interests me. I'm curious about this whole process of
taming a feral cat—or trying to. How will he react to the
techniques I can figure out—even if it's just visiting with
him, sleeping in his room some nights? What will make
him love *me* when he resists other people? Can I seduce
him into being affectionate with me? I'll be patient. I
don't think he wants to run away. No indeed. He wants to
rest safely under his bed and let himself heal.

I know how he feels. Or think I do. Oh, that time I got
fired from my job in the career counseling office! Back
in the eighties. What a nightmare. Why is it that people
like me, who bat about in life, think they can give college
kids advice about their futures? Maybe we like to imagine ourselves in all the potential careers we sketch out
for the students: doctor, lawyer, artist. Maybe we like to
live different lives vicariously. But I had the boss from
hell and I acted like the employee from hell—too bloody
outspoken. God, I shudder to think the kinds of things
I said. At one point, when my boss wouldn't let me hold
a month-long career workshop just for English majors,
I actually told her, "You are in my way!" But I felt per-
secuted and it was horrible. After I'd finally worked out
a deal to leave there, I drove up to Maine for a week.
Lucky me to have a dear college roommate with a house
near the water—not to mention a gracious husband and
two children under the age of ten. I sat on their porch,

drank wine, gossiped about college friends, and read mystery stories. In the afternoons, I took long walks into town with the kids—including my much beloved godson. We loaded up sacks of penny candy and then wandered home eating strawberry Twizzlers on a road where the scent of pine litter rose hot and spicy from the dust. I slept late and went to bed early. In short, my wounds healed. When I arrived back home after that magic week I felt revved up, ready to search for a job more suitable to a freethinker.

Maybe that's what's going on under the bed. Henry's having a week in Maine.

Tuesday, April 15, Payday (at last!) and Tax Day

Lucille sat in bed with me this morning and purred and purred—a full, deep-throated, happy purr. The white spot under her chin throbbed with satisfaction. She's glad she doesn't have to share my bed with that cat upstairs! It took two years for her to start to purr after she came to live with me. Since I'd never had a cat before, I didn't know a lot about purring. It never occurred to me that she should hum with pleasure now and then. She didn't frolic around much either. She'd lived with me for a whole month before I saw her play—tapping at red Christmas balls that hung from the tree. She's been very loving since Henry came. Andy says she's sucking up.

When I finally climbed the stairs up to his room and pushed my face under the bed to see him, Henry seemed to favor his right eye. He looked as if he didn't want to open it and he kept dimming his left eye also. Did the car strike his head when it hit him? On Henry's second day in the hospital, Dr. Royster had worried that tires might have caused a brain injury. Was this eye problem an after-effect of his run-in with a truck or even a tractor? My heart caught at the idea.

As soon as I got to work, I called the vet. In his reassuring voice, Dr. Royster told me not to worry about Henry's brain. His eye thing couldn't be from the accident; that had happened too long ago. He said we should just hope it resolves itself—or maybe I could rub some salve on it. After putting down the phone, I propped my head in my hands, spreading my elbows on the steel desk. Salve? What was he thinking? I stared into space for a few moments. Then I went across the hall to Andy's office in the graphics department, squinched down on the floor next to her desk, and told her about the salve. She leaned down, spreading her Pantone color deck out in front of me like a fan. "Which do you like, the blue or the teal?"

"Teal. I always like teal." I didn't even know what brochure she was working on. She laid the deck on her desk and looked at me. "God help you if you have to rub ointment onto that cat."

"How on earth would I do it? Cradle him in my arms?"

"It's an ambitious project. Taming Henry."

"C'mon. I can't even get near him."

For once she had no useful advice, but at least she understood the problem.

Friday, April 25

Vacation day. In my garden, morning sun slanted along the wall and stroked my arm. Railroad horns and an announcer on a loudspeaker at the Penn Relay races across the river in West Philly sounded oddly companionable. The sounds give a feeling of depth, of distance, although the river flows only a few blocks away. The Schuylkill—hard to spell. I'm told it's Dutch for "Hidden River," which is what it might as well be for me. I keep wanting to find it, to walk by it as I used to do when I lived in Germantown and wandered down to East River Drive. There it's easy to find; you just park in one of the laybys and meander down to the banks. I loved strolling along, watching scullers racing under the bridges, smelling wet leaves under the willows that hang over the stream. But to get to the stretch of water that's only blocks from my new house, I apparently have to go down some steps, which I haven't found yet—even though I've tried. I've gone to Judy Garland Park—so called 'cause gay guys cruise there—which lies on higher ground above the river. I know the water shimmers somewhere near, but I can't find the steps. The banks of this tidal stretch, which flows into the Delaware, lie undeveloped, although I keep reading about plans to put a bike trail down there. Well, a project for another day—finding the river. How can you not find a river? It's craziness.

Speaking of which. Last night, determined to touch him, I terrorized Henry, poor lamb. As long as he could scoot around under the double bed, my arms couldn't reach him. So I dismantled his hideaway, taking off the roof—which is to say the mattress and box springs. He ran in terror and flung himself against the window. He's clearly OK physically. Then he crouched in a corner. All the while, talking sweetly, I crept closer and closer. He hissed and spat a foul odor—but finally I put my right hand, wrapped in a towel, on his surprisingly plump body. Then, at last, holding him with my right hand still in the towel, I rested my left hand on his warm head and scratched behind his ears until his fur parted beneath my thumb. He didn't make a sound. Then I patted his soft, submissive head. After backing away, I put his safe haven together again and mushed tasty Fancy Feast tuna in his dish. Is it my imagination, or is he looking darts and daggers at me today?

May

Thursday, May 1

Yesterday, Andy told me I should make my hand into a sort of paw—putting crunchy kibble between my fingers—and see if Henry will take the food. So tonight I tried it. Squinched down on my stomach, I scattered a few tuna-flavored pebbles on the back of my hand and very slowly slid it toward his face. He didn't move a muscle for a full minute. Then I edged my paw right under his chin. He looked down, darted his pink tongue out and scarfed up three or four kibbles. Then he got up, humped his back against the box springs and sat upright. He'd finished his snack.

Once again I wondered if he'd had any experience of humans. Why is he still so frightened? Did someone hurt him? Was he running away when I picked him up in the road? Andy told me about her abused bird, called—for whatever reason—Cookie. Apparently it took Cookie forever to come around—and some mornings she still won't let Andy touch her. I can imagine Henry skulking about the house when he's been here for five years. I sure hope he gets friendlier or I'll have invested all this time and energy and kept this journal and he'll still be undomesticated. It's more than that, of course. I feel waves of affection for the little guy. I want him to forget his troubles—whatever they were. I want to hold and comfort him, reassure him that he's safe with me. That we're both safe.

All the more reason to be thankful that I don't have to smear salve in his eye. He's no longer favoring it, so whatever bothered him has cleared up. One problem solved.

I feel guilty about keeping the door to his room closed. Why can't I just leave it open until he comes out—a day or so later? Well, I'm too lazy to cat-proof the house and I'm afraid of what he might do. Probably, he would just hiss at Lucille, hide behind a sofa or under the antique chest, and come out five nights later. What about the basement? What kind of trouble could he get into down there? I hate to think about these things. The real problem is that, if I leave his door open, I'll have to keep the garden doors closed day and night. I've always hated closed-in places, gates, limits of any kind. But if he got out into the garden, he'd be gone.

Last night, I dreamed about a version of Henry. He looked like a little lemony kitten, about four months old, frolicking around at a surreal party with strangers. Adults in green headscarves chatted with me while Henry played with some children. He jumped around, darting among the kids' legs. Even in the dream, an empty feeling slid along my arms every time he seemed to disappear. Clearly, one reason I keep him locked up is that I'm afraid of losing him.

Sunday, May 11

Bright and sparkling. This morning, at Home Depot—
Home Despot, Andy calls it—I picked out new peren-
nials for the garden: fragrant forget-me-nots and shrub
roses. My neighbor Cathy Crimmins came by when I was
unloading the car. She scooped up a potted white rose
with one long arm and held onto her new puppy's leash
with the other. Once inside the house, she dropped the
leash. The puppy darted around the rug, undoubtedly
smelling Lucille, while Cathy brought the plant through
my living room and plopped it down on my brick patio.
She's at least a foot taller than I and she smiled down on
me, saying how cool the white flowers would look against
my stucco wall. Flash memories of the huge grapevine
that snakes around Cathy and Alan's backyard a block
away kept coming into my mind. Every fall we "harvest"
it in a grape-stomping party when Cathy crushes the fruit
under her feet in a child's plastic blowup pool. She liked
my choice, thank heaven. I can never be sure with Cathy.
She seems to accrue all the glamour and style to herself.

The new puppy appeared on the garden doorstep,
wagging his entire body. He's a little Jack Russell Terrier
called Silver. He sports two round spots on his back—
one right in front of his tail. Cathy pointed out that it
wiggles when his tail wags. We went back into my living
room and sat on the floor with him. He's soft as satin. He
climbed up my legs and licked my face. When Lucille
came in, they sniffed and rubbed noses. Lucille hissed at
him, but he still wanted to make friends. After a while,
she wandered off, probably thinking the puppy faintly

ridiculous. However, this little encounter proved she could at least tolerate another creature. Cathy says she wishes Silver were a cat so she could just point him to the litter box and say, "Get with the program, dude."

Late this afternoon I went out to plant the roses, digging my very small patch of earth with my spade. The arch of my foot pushed the sharp metal deep into the soil—very satisfying, even through the layers of thick skin on my feet. The shrubs will grace my wall with white blossoms, easy to see in the evening when I get home from work. After I'd finished, I hitched up my jeans, scratched my midriff, leaned my spade against the back wall, and came inside, leaving the garden door open. I couldn't bear to close it with all the spring scents coming in—cherry blossoms from my neighbor across the back wall, peonies from the pot right outside my garden door, the honeysuckle vine beginning to spiral around the telephone wires that snake along the side of my house. So I sat on the sofa, reading, with the night air breezing in, beginning to feel more at home in my house, beginning to feel it's my own. Maybe I'm just plain getting used to it. Lucille meandered out into the garden but I didn't freak out, didn't even get up to watch her. I just sat there, enjoying the peaceful hour. After a while, she came back in, gave me a loud meow, and walked over to get a drink of water from her bowl on the kitchen floor. When she came back into the living room, she sat looking at me for a moment and then hopped up on the wing chair, circled several times, and finally dropped into a perfect curl. Am I becoming less afraid of losing her? Is it because of

Henry upstairs? Because he's there? A kind of spare cat, like Prince Harry's a spare king? Never mind—she's clearly not about to leave me.

Monday, May 12

I'm frankly discouraged about Henry. I need help. This is an adult wild cat with well-developed instincts for protecting his den.

Last week, bit by bit, I changed his environment. One day, I took the mattress off his bed again and leaned it against the wall. With a pile of clean towels and his own dust ruffle, I rigged up a new hiding place in a closet—small enough for me to reach in to pat his fat little rump. Two days later, the box springs came off. Henry clearly had scouted the alternative lair. He scooted over to the closet, arched his back, hissed, and spat. For about forty-five minutes—without ever trying to touch him—I sat right there on the carpet with my legs crossed, reading a magazine and blinking my eyes at my wild creature.

In the night, he found the triangle behind the chest of drawers that stands at an angle to the corner walls. This morning I found him in this place of his own choosing, hissing and spitting. With this setup, it's easier to wriggle closer to him than it was when he scurried around under the bed. I'll have to crawl to get near him because if I stand tall over him he'll be scared, but I can probably slide near enough to put his collar on.

This morning when he hissed and spat at me I told him he might have to go to "the farmer." "The farmer" is an imaginary guy with a big spread and lots of barn cats where Henry could go and enjoy a happy life if he never gets used to living with me in the city. "The farmer's other cats would pick on you," I said, "because you don't have any balls anymore!" He seemed contrite. He probably knows this is an idle threat. What farmer would have him? How would I get him there?

Still, I'd better call Dr. Royster and try to get an understanding of the time it takes to domesticate a wild cat so Henry and I will know what we're in for.

Tuesday, May 13

Henry now favors the triangle behind the chest of drawers where the walls come together in a corner—probably because he picked it himself. He pokes his head out of this place and peers at the world. He doesn't always hiss when I go up there. Sometimes he blinks his green eyes at me most fetchingly. Maybe he can just sit there till he slowly gets used to things.

Am I imagining it, or did Henry not want me to leave last night? As I backed out with my hand on the door, his pupils got wider and wider and he jutted his pointy head up toward me. I couldn't make myself pull the iron handle tight and shut out this picture. So I decided to leave it open an inch or two. Tiptoeing down the stairs, I half expected him to streak by and make a run for his freedom. But I didn't hear a sound.

This morning I went upstairs first thing with my heart in my mouth. Would he still be there? But the door stood cracked open just as I'd left it. Surely if Henry had bolted he wouldn't have turned around and pulled the door almost closed behind him. I slipped in, walked over to the chest of drawers and leaned my head behind it, nerving myself to find an empty towel. But Henry just looked up at me and licked his chops, ready for breakfast.

Saturday, May 17

Last night, Henry came out from his room for sure. He got as far as the cool, dry shower stall in the upstairs bathroom. That's where he is right this minute. At least I think so. This morning, when I climbed up to see him, he wasn't lurking in his familiar place behind the chest of drawers. His toys lay scattered about his room and his shoestring slithered on the hallway floor in front of the yellow bookcase—evidence that he'd been moving about. Had he been playing in the night? Or wildly running about up and down the stairs? I looked all over the house, becoming more and more panicky, but then I heard Andy's voice in my head, saying, "Oh, Anne, he hasn't gone far." I tried the bathroom again. Behind the shower curtain, he lay curled around the drain, enjoying his new hiding place. At least he has a change of scene and doesn't feel locked in.

Five minutes later...

Henry's gone back to his lair behind the yellow chest of drawers in the corner of the bedroom. Just now I went upstairs, expecting to see him in the shower stall, but he had obviously thought better of it and retreated to a place of greater safety.

It's two months to the day since I picked Henry up in the road. Hurray for Henry! He's alive and warm and beginning to explore.

Tuesday, May 27

Total Henry trauma last weekend.

On Sunday morning, an hour before I left to catch the train north for the Yale graduation, I went looking for Henry. Couldn't find him anywhere. He wasn't under the bed, or behind the chest of drawers, or in the shower stall. I scoured the house, opened all the closet doors, looked under sofas, on top of bookcases, even in the basement boiler room. Did he get out into the garden when I left the back door open last night? I didn't want to leave him, but what could I do? My godson was graduating from Yale. The same godson who had walked with me on dusty roads in Maine, eating strawberry Twizzlers when he was ten years old. I had to go. After putting two huge green ceramic mixing bowls of cat food and water on the kitchen floor, I left the garden door open a crack. Thank God there's no alley, so no one can come in when I'm away except the people who live in the complex. In the pouring rain, which mixed with my tears, I ran around the block to alert the neighbors that an orange cat was missing. Then I called Andy. She comforted me. "If he really went," she said, "that's where he wants to be."

Sitting on the train to New Haven, I fought down visions of Henry lost in the rain, hiding under cars, drenched like the orange cat called Cat in *Breakfast at Tiffany's* when Audrey Hepburn throws him out of the taxi. I didn't even try to tell myself that Henry's only a cat. I felt I'd deserted him. It would be an unbearable two days before I could look for him again. I wanted to get off the train at Trenton and go back. Go back and find him, put my nose next to that wet little triangle on the end of his snout, rub my thumb behind his ear. But it's my godson, right? He'd be disappointed if I didn't show up. So for a while I stared at the white pocketbook in my lap, utterly miserable. I felt completely trapped until a bit of Jersey sun seemed to warm the black plastic piping around the window next to my seat. Slowly, I began to look up and look out. By the time we passed New York, I'd grown calmer. I began to realize that Henry had recovered. That he looked strong, well-nourished. Better than when I picked him up.

Yale put on a classic graduation—heavy male influence at Mory's for dinner the night before the ceremony, flags and banners in the Old Campus on commencement day, a young white woman singing a lovely Swahili blessing at Davenport College where the new graduate beamed for the camera. Of course I remembered when my Yalie godson's mother and I graduated from college on a rainy day thirty years ago. It's good to have these long friendships and it's good for me, with no husband or children of my own, to have godsons and nephews like Tommy. Sometimes it feels easier to talk to them than to their parents. The kids, especially when very young, seem so openly imaginative. I remember an evening when Liz, who now accepts Tommy's adoration as his older sister, was a brilliant three-year-old. After dinner one night she said calmly, "Annie, let's go outside to see what the moon's thinking." What an intriguing thing to say. And young people can be so generous. I hadn't said a word about Henry to anyone, not wanting to spoil things—and thinking that a lost stray cat hardly rated in comparison with the glories of Yale graduation. But after the ceremonies I found myself at lunch next to Nora, today consigned to being merely the graduate's younger sister. Nora has a long history with cats, most especially a very smart tabby called Nica, her childhood companion. I figured Nora would understand, so I told her about Henry. She leaned down toward me, pulled her shiny chestnut hair behind her ears. She's nineteen and she's stunning. Unconscious of her beauty for a moment, she looked directly at me. "Oh Annie, you must be so worried." Her eyes widened. Then she drew herself upright. "When you get back, you'll find him, you will. Then you must call me. Absolutely." Not for the last time, I felt grateful to Nora for her insight and her rather blunt kindness.

The minute I got home I started searching for Henry—this time slowly, room by room, from the top of the house down. On the third floor, I peered into the farthest reaches of the closets, under the bed, behind the red wing chair. No Henry. Then I went down to look between the mattress and box springs of my bed on the second floor. Not there. In the kitchen, the cabinets held only dishes and crackers and musty jars of spices. Nothing but dust bunnies behind the fridge. Finally, only the cellar was left. Walking down the basement stairs one by one, I turned to my right where the air conditioning vent runs along unfinished ceiling beams. Two blond paws stood on top of the vent. I tiptoed down another step until his green eyes appeared. He looked at me, hissed, and spat with a foul odor. Man, was I excited to see that bad boy!

June

Saturday, June 21

Hot, hot, hot. Thick heat buffets my garden walls but the tropical plants flourish. They think it's Miami with all this heat—not Center City Philadelphia, for heaven's sake. Even in the early morning, Lucille stayed sprawled on the cool linoleum kitchen floor. She hasn't been messing with Henry at all. I guess she thinks it's too hot to do anything.

Tommy came to hang out today. After I picked him up at his house, we went to Zany Brainy, the "intellectual" toy store. In the car, feeling a little like a cheapskate but knowing how fast the tab for kids' toys can add up, I explained the one-gift-per-child rule again, but Tommy seemed to accept the terms just fine. He hopped out of the car and I followed him in. It's a lovely open place, dotted with primary colors. Tommy clearly knows the layout. He slid down the aisles past games, electronic toys, and CDs. We paused at the video booth, where three little kids watched *Sesame Street*. Apparently you can buy a video and enjoy Big Bird whenever you want. But Tommy didn't linger. He ran on, coming to a halt in front of the Lego aisle. Of course. He has an extensive Lego kingdom laid out on the floor of his room at home. Castles and seas spill out from his domain and into the hallway. Fat round pirates with rubbery swords lie about on the stairs. Standing in Zany Brainy's aisle, we conferred about which set to buy—but not for long. I think he had his mind made up before we ever walked into the store. A new pirate ship, with about a thousand pieces, was just the ticket. In its shiny box, it stood at eye level for him. While he reached it down, he ticked off the highlights. "The Cross Bone Clipper. It's got two pirate flags and a cannon."

"Excellent!" I was getting into this. "All the better to kill off the British."

"Cannon softens 'em up. Then we knock 'em off with cutlasses. Like Jimmy." Ah, Jimmy—the boy hero of the story I wrote for Tommy last Christmas. Jimmy's a decidedly bloodthirsty child who joins the pirates and swings into action with his cutlass. He's personally responsible for at least five British deaths. Tommy and I loved it. I recorded it on a cassette for him, complete with appropriate sound effects. He listened to the tape every night before falling asleep—causing the occasional nightmare, according to his father.

We wandered away from the Lego aisle toward the checkout lanes, but I got sidetracked at a corner display filled with puppets. Tommy watched as I tried on a praying mantis and, even better, a gray rat with pink ears, a pink nose, and white whiskers. I scrunched up his face with my fingers and made the rat nibble Tommy's ear. Tommy looked at me out of the corner of his eye and said, "Annie wants to be a child." I couldn't dispute it. I'm afraid I bought both the rat and the mantis—totally ignoring the one-gift-per-child rule. We put our treasures in the car and went off to Minella's diner for toasted cheese sandwiches, both of us pleased as punch with our new toys.

In the afternoon, Tommy and I joined Cathy and her daughter Kelly in an excursion to the piney woods in South Jersey, where we swam in the muddy cold water of a creek. Tommy seemed a little wary of Kelly at first, even though he's got two years on her.

Maybe he thinks she's unpredictable. Cathy and I played the role of children in this scenario, splashing in the cold stream, dreaming of finding a summer shack nearby. The real kids sat chatting on a tree root while Cathy and I swam under heavy green branches. "Hey, Kel," she yelled, "don't ja wanna swing on the willow and jump in?"

Kelly eyed the tree. Its sinuous branches danced above the slippery bank, slick with wet leaves. She's used to her mom's slightly dangerous ideas. She and Tommy decided to stay put. After a while, I climbed out and sat on my haunches next to them. Crickets all around mingled their tenor vibes with the shriek of planes at McGuire Air Force Base but the crickets, rich in the lush air, prevailed. I want to be in a place like this: open, the woods. I want it now. Sick of the city. All the noise. Being locked up.

Cathy splashed around in the deepest part of the creek for a while like some great frog, all big arms and legs, totally in her element. I pulled on a willow branch, stripping the leaves. "Hey, Cathy, do you know where the Schuylkill River is? I mean, how to get to it, walk down there from our neighborhood?"

Treading water, she made lazy swirls with her hands, which looked almost transparent. "Get to it?"

"Yeah. Where the steps are? The bridge." I clasped

my breasts with my arms, rocked a little on my haunches. "How you get from Pine Street to the actual water. So
you can walk along it?"

"Sure."

"Will ya show me?"

She grinned all over her round Irish face. "Sure."

"Excellent." I stretched, holding my fists against my
ears for a moment, then settled on the bank.

"I take Silver for runs down there. All the time." She
lifted her head, took a huge swallow of air, and dove right
back into the weedy creek.

Maybe she actually will take me there some afternoon. After all, it's only a block from her house, two
blocks from mine. Our neighborhood stretch of river.
Still hidden, as far as I'm concerned.

I'm writing this while Tommy—and the praying
mantis—are, I trust, asleep in Henry's room. When we
went in, Henry stayed silently under the bed. I guess he
thinks it's safer to stay in deep cover in his old quarters
rather than cower behind his dresser when someone un-
familiar is in the room. Tommy lay on his stomach in his
Care Bear pajamas and tried to play with him, but Henry
was having none of it. I heard some hissing while I turned
down the bedspread. Tommy gave up pretty soon and
climbed into bed. I kissed him good night, left the night-
light on, and came down here to the living room.

Lovely to have Tommy in the house. I wish a child
lived with me here, someone soft, familiar, companionable. Of course, this is unrealistic in the extreme. But I
love simply being with someone quietly. Tommy doesn't
talk a lot these days—unless it's to give important infor-

mation about cannons. He just doesn't feel like it, perhaps. He thinks his own thoughts. And I don't push him too far. He can talk if and when he wants to. But I'll figure out more ways of hanging out with Tommy—excursions and such. He does seem to like being around me. Hey, who wouldn't like an indulgent aunt?

Friday, June 27

Henry doesn't hiss or spit much anymore. In fact, he meowed in a treble this morning when kibble clattered into his dish under the bed, where he still hides out now and then. He stretched, lagging his left leg behind, and then trotted up to get his food. He even ate it while I peered in at him. Lovely butterscotch markings ring his legs. After breakfast, he washed his face, tilting his head and drawing his paw up over his ears again and again as I've seen Lucille do a hundred times. Quite a normal cat, really.

Andy and I took our lunch to the atrium today. The fiendish architect who designed our windowless offices redeemed himself—or thought he had redeemed himself—by putting a light-filled space in the middle of the building with a tiny cafeteria shoehorned into a corner. Maybe the cafeteria was Mr. Macaleer's idea. Thrifty entrepreneur that he is, he doesn't want his employees to waste valuable time leaving the building for lunch. He shows up himself now and then and waits in line with the rest of us, even though he's the CEO.

Andy always brings leftovers from home. Today she spooned red bell pepper sauce over spinach pasta. She offered me a bite when I leaned in to smell that roasted pepper fragrance. I only wanted to tell her about Henry, about how he held his left paw out last night and licked it right in front of me, but she'd heard I was writing a script for a new sales video. "Pretty hot stuff," she said. "Expensive proposition. Film production." She licked her spoon. "Who's coming up with the money?" Project funding always causes problems, but I've become shameless about persuading managers that video helps with sales. I think I even used the words "Return On Investment."

"Sales meeting budget. Frank Lavelle's pocket." I slipped into my best Hollywood voice. "Head Sales Manager debuts shiny new video. Whips up troops."

"You convinced Frank to part with cash?"

"Let's just say I'm reliably informed he'll pony up."

"Tell him his sales reps only learn by looking." She took a bite of her whole-grain roll. "At videos."

"God knows they don't read." Andy's strictly a print designer, so I changed the topic. "Tell me about those beautiful brain scan photos you found."

She looked over at the potted calla lilies. "You're sure you want to slap a brain scan on a direct mail piece?"

"Sure. Totally jazzy."

We talked logistics for a while and then I harangued her about how our piece would doubtless bring in lots of business for our healthcare sales reps. I told her Frank and the other managers would shower us with fruit baskets at Christmas. She inspected her cookie. "Dream on," she said.

While she licked the chocolate chips, we got around to Henry. "He spoke to me this morning," I told her, fingering the string of green glass beads that had belonged to my grandmother.

"What did he say?" she asked. Her Tupperware container snapped shut.

"Meow."

"Asking for his breakfast. You were probably late. Falling behind."

"Do you think he roams around the house at night? I leave the door to his room open."

"Your entire place is his kingdom."

She seemed to have a lifetime of experience with cats. I felt like a novice. "Yes, but—"

Her dark eyes caught mine. "Look, Anne, he does what he wants. Your job is to feed him and keep him safe." She put her hands together on the white table. "You're doing your job." As we walked back to our offices, I wondered how I would keep him safe if he started to go out into the garden.

July

Tuesday, July 8

Henry ran up and down the stairs like crazy last night. It sounded like burglars in the house. Maybe he was just horny or feeling his oats. But he's been banging against the window in his room again. It's held, but I need to go to the hardware store and buy some kind of glue to seal it. There's no screen and God knows I don't want him to fall three stories. Another window sealed—how I hate being closed in!

If he's going to carouse up and down the stairs and maybe go out into my garden—particularly if I ever put a cat flap in the back door—I'm gonna have to get his collar and his nametag on him. This could be a trauma for him and for me. A tender, fragile thread of trust has been developing between us every time he eats from my hand-dish or lets me give him a stroke on his whiskery blond face. What will the effect be if I chase him down, throw a towel around his plump, hissing self, and put a collar round his neck? It'll set us back two weeks.

Even if he has his collar on, I'll have to get used to him coming and going. I'm such a possessive person; I'll worry and fret. I'll be afraid that he doesn't really care for me, that I haven't seduced him thoroughly enough. That he'll wander off and get friendly with the neighbor lady and want to stay with her. Then I'll think fondly of the days when I could count on finding him underneath his bed—young and kittenish and happy to eat his dinner between my fingers.

Friday, July 11

Meanwhile, there's a Portuguese cat called "Vasco da Gama" living next door for a few days. Neighbor Priscilla adores cats but her husband Fred is allergic, so it's quite a treat for Priscilla, who gardens in a denim skirt, to have Vasco nosing around while she waters the hostas. He arrived with Priscilla's sister, who just came home from a stint with the Foreign Service in Portugal and needs to leave Vasco here until she finds a new house in Washington. How did she get Vasco through quarantine? I guess the Foreign Service thing helps. Anyway, Vasco seems quite friendly and, like his namesake, explores. He climbs up and down the tree between Priscilla and Fred's house and mine. He will probably come over, stroll in through the garden door, and terrorize Henry.

In the evenings I've been sitting in a white plastic chair on my Juliet balcony so I can keep an eye on Vasco's activities. On clear nights I can see the moon, although the city lights obscure the stars. I love watching the big spruce tree a block over on Waverly Street. It sways its stubby branches even on ordinary windy nights; it's even more dramatic in a thunderstorm. Sitting on my balcony, I have a view down into South Philly. Philadelphia is such a low city. Not many skyscrapers. When I look south, in fact, there's not a high-rise to be seen— just strict rows of three-story brick and stucco houses, interspersed with street trees. It's the kind of vista I like, with depth of field, a sense of distance. Last night I was lingering there, admiring it and drinking a glass of wine, when Henry nosed his way out onto the balcony doorstep. He didn't say anything but sat with his head halfway out the door, his paws underneath his chest. We sat quite companionably, listening to the crickets. A lovely country-in-the-city scene.

Sunday, July 13

Lucille is in love with the Portuguese cat—or so it seems to me. He paraded along the wall and she sat in my flowers and they made deep calling sounds to each other. It's a cry unlike any other I've ever heard her make. Then she flung herself against the yew tree trunk trying to get to him. She fell back—no front claws—breaking my grandmother's goblet I'd left on a side table.

Vasco da Gama—called "Vachoo," so Priscilla tells me—looked inquisitively and Lucille tried again to get a grip on the wall, the yew tree, anything that would get her to him—but she kept falling back. Eventually Vasco got discouraged, I guess, turned around, and dropped off the wall into Priscilla's garden. Well, it's good for Lucille to have a European admirer. I do think they wanted to meet. It didn't sound territorial. Then again, maybe they were caterwauling. Maybe she didn't want him anywhere near her garden and told him so in terms that he understood and that I, of course, did not. Yikes. What do I know about cats? I'd better look it up in a book or call Andy and humble myself, yet again.

Monday, July 21

Vasco the Portuguese cat has gone with Priscilla's sister to his new home in Washington—and Lucille has lost her beau, or whatever he was. Maybe she just successfully defended her domain even without front claws. Problem is, now she's staking out her territory against Henry. They fight like cats and dogs these days. Even I can see that Lucille is protecting her turf and Henry wants in. This morning about six thirty, while I thrashed under my new African-patterned cotton quilt, she went downstairs for reasons of her own. Meanwhile, Henry skittered in under my bed and staked out a corner. I tried to go back to sleep. A little later, Lucille padded up the stairs and marched in. As I leaned over to watch, she crept under the box springs, her tail disappearing last. Is it my imagination or does she look thinner? Maybe she's losing weight, what with all this fighting. I nerved myself for trouble, but for a while an unreal calm prevailed. Sleep seemed possible. Then Henry started hissing, Lucille growled, and the two of them spat and shrieked at each other until I lumbered to my feet and yelled, "Enough!" Lucille slid out from under the bed and slowly left the room, holding her tail down low and her dignity as high as she could.

As I went downstairs to make coffee, Henry followed, passing me on the steps and sprinting into the kitchen. While I waited for the kettle to boil, scratching the back of my neck and hearing sirens in the street again, Lucille came in, cool as a cucumber with her tail stuck up in the air, and hissed at him in passing. He ran straight out of the room. She walked directly over to her water bowl and commenced slurping. So sometimes she still gets the upper hand. But what happens if they get into a knock-down, drag-out fight? He might hurt her with those talons. I'll have to protect her as best I can, especially since I'm the fool who had her declawed in front—just to protect the damn furniture. God knows I'll never do that to another cat, least of all my wild Henry—as if I could get close enough to grab him, stuff him into a cat carrier, and haul him off to some back alley vet. But what if he were to run away? It would break my heart, but at least I'd know he could defend himself against any fierce city cats.

August

Monday, August 11

Hazy. Hot. Thick weather. Rain coming.

Henry and Lucille have come to a truce. Last night he stole into my bedroom, sliding in along the wall. When he saw Lucille, he bowed his head and she held her front paw between his ears. She's a little dominatrix! He hasn't conquered her yet. He slept under my bed and Lucille slept on her pillow next to me. He tried to come up onto the white sheets once, but Lucille hissed him off. She's defending her last bastion to the bitter end. I love her and comfort her and stroke her but I feel like I'm betraying her. Hopefully, she'll come to understand that Henry can sleep at the bottom of the bed and she can sleep on her pillow next to me.

Certainly these cats amuse me. Even their territorial negotiations—if I can call them that—intrigue me. And I love the very dailyness of having them around. Saying hello to Henry as he pads past me on the stairs, intent on going down to the kitchen for a snack. Asking Lucille if she's coming in or staying out when she hesitates at the garden door on a winter afternoon. I love all the to-ing and fro-ing—the small commotions in the house, the sense of living my life alongside two other lives, with creatures who have their own ideas about things. Is it a substitute for family life? Perhaps. Though I think I'm clear about the difference between kids and cats. But all this activity in my house, the cats' quirky ways, and even their bickering—all this brings a liveliness to my home that I enjoy. They also give me bodily warmth, the downright comfort of being touched. They don't care if my skin is dry. I still feed Henry with my hand just to feel his whiskers tingle my fingers and his soft tongue rasp my palm.

This afternoon I called Dr. Royster to bring him up to date and to say thanks for the night I brought Henry to him and found a welcome and kind hands. Dr. Royster told me that a friend of his had a wild stray cat who took eleven months to come around and really trust her. I asked him if his friend had any other cats. He said no, but he told me to give Henry and Lucille time. "They probably have issues to work out," he said. He got that right.

Sunday, August 17

It's five months to the day since I picked Henry up in the road—what a salvation that was! He's a handsome, stout cat. Runs like lightning!

Last night Henry must have followed Lucille into the garden, although he's never been out there before—that I know of. At about six o'clock I cracked the back door open for Lucille and left to go to a party. When I got home, Henry was nowhere to be seen. Then I thought to look outside. I switched on the garden light and spotted him near the wall, rummaging among the ferns where Lucille likes to sit. She eyed him from the breezy table. She whiffed a little, as if it hurt her to breathe, but then she hopped down and went into the house. He lingered, sniffing worms and slugs, his ears cocked forward. Before bed, I wandered into the garden again and peered at him neatly curled in the ferns with one paw covering his snout. He opened an eye, raised his head, stood up, broke cover, scooted in, and ran upstairs. No question but that he knew exactly how to get back inside. So maybe he *has* been in the garden before. If the cats could speak English, or even French, they'd tell me a thing or two to calm my worries—or make me worry even more.

Monday, August 18

This morning, I determined to get Henry's collar on him—for his own protection, right? If he got lost, my phone number on his nametag might bring him back to me.

Up in his lair behind the chest of drawers, he sat with his paws tucked under his chest, peering at me. "If you are going roaming, young man, you'll need to have a collar." He looked unconcerned. I put his food between my fingers and pushed my paw toward him on the carpet. He kneaded, purred, and licked the kibble up with his soft tongue. But when I raised my hand to catch him he drew back, scooted behind me, and put his head into his yellow dish to scarf up some more breakfast. I began to realize that there was no sense in playing havoc with his trust. After a bit, he began to rub his scent onto a bamboo wastebasket, wiping his head against it. Then he wandered over in my direction. I fed him again with my hand, though he wasn't quite as trustful this time. I left the collar on the floor. If he strays, it's more likely he'll come back to a soft touch.

So there it is. Henry is given to posing on the stairs between the second and third floors these days. His green eyes match the green carpet and I'm sure he's quite aware of how handsome he is. Come to think of it, his eyes are sort of the same color as mine, only mine are more hazel, with flecks of amber in the irises. I'm told it's an unusual color, hazel. Hard to describe. Hard to pin down. Always shifting. Elusive—that's me, eh?

Sunday, August 24

Miss Lucille is having trouble breathing. I finally got worried enough to take her to see Dr. Royster yesterday morning. I also brought along a photo of Henry sitting on the green stairs. In the waiting room, while I looked up at the bulletin board showing snapshots of Dr. Royster's patients—all the cured cats and dogs and birds—Lucille sat quietly on my lap. She never stirs from my arms, so I don't worry about stuffing her in a carrier though I probably should get one. A friendly golden retriever came up and sniffed her, but she didn't make a sound. I confess I felt very pleased at being so protective of her. When we got back to the green examining room, Dr. Royster held her firmly and felt her innards. I told him about her difficulty breathing. With his thumbs, he palpated her throat. "Has she been drinking a lot?" he asked.

"Not so very much, I guess. But I do fill the water bowl more often."

"Running around? Hyperactive?"

"She fights with Henry. You know, the rescued cat. All the time."

He patted Lucille and went to wash his hands in the little white basin. "It's territorial. She's not sure about the new guy."

Tensing up myself, I stroked Lucille's back. My mouth seemed to be hanging open, waiting for his verdict. I always feel rather childish in doctor's offices. Dr. Royster asked me if he could run some blood tests, and of course I agreed. When he'd drawn her blood, he labeled the vial and turned around to face me. "I'm concerned about hyperthyroidism. The tests will let us know." His voice seemed to get farther and farther away as he went on to tell me that medicine could treat Lucille's problem. I surfaced at the words "Put a pill in her food every day."

"A pill. In her food." I had a vision of forcing fat pink lozenges through Lucille's clenched teeth. Then I thought of tuna fish. "Can I grind it up and mix it with tuna juice?"

He laughed a deep, lingering laugh. "You can do it however you want."

"OK, Lucille." I caressed her behind her ears. "Tuna juice. Every single day. Yum."

"Don't let's get ahead of ourselves," he said. "But I think that's what it is. I'll call you with the test results in a few days." He explained that hyperthyroidism is not uncommon in older cats. That the treatment could keep it under control and she could live a fairly normal life. Of course I wondered how serious this was, how close I was to losing her, but I was afraid to ask. Maybe I didn't want to know. All I wanted was to look after her, and protect her, and keep her with me for as long as I could. And anyway, I had Henry. My other cat. My spare.

Dr. Royster, who's a handsome man in his thirties, paused for a moment with his hand on the door while I drew the photo of Henry out of my pocket and showed it to him. "He finally came out from under the bed," I said. Dr. Royster admired Henry's pose, but he didn't seem surprised.

"Are these your stairs?" he asked, slipping the photo into his lab coat side pocket.

"So to speak. Mainly they're Henry's stairs."

He leaned back against the doorjamb. "How's life in the big city?" He always wants to know about the coolest new restaurants. Clearly, he's a hip guy—always beautifully dressed with a blue tartan tie or something like that. Although he presumably needs to live close to his practice, I secretly think he's got a yearning for city life. Maybe he hopes to move his family into town someday.

"You should try Dmitri's cafe." I gathered Lucille up in my arms. "On Catharine Street."

"She'll stay in your arms?"

"Yeah. Always does." I stroked her leg with my thumb, stared at his Tuskegee Vet School diploma hanging on the cinderblock. "I guess I'm getting used to the city. By now." I kept my eyes on the wall, looking beyond him—always a sign I'm not sure about something. Then I put my friendly face on again, which is not hard to do with him. "Dimitri makes fabulous grilled octopus. You'd love it."

He smiled broadly, suggested I get a carrier, and left with the vial in his top pocket.

Tuesday, August 26

6:30 p.m. Tonight may be the beginning of a new chapter in my relationship with cats. Trusting they won't willingly leave. That they're content with me. It may also be the last time I ever see Henry Kaier. Right now he's perched on top of my garden wall, sitting on the ivy vine.

While I lingered in the doorway a few minutes ago, smelling the honeysuckle, something rustled in the dark leaves. Probably just a squirrel. But as I moved closer, Henry settled his haunches on the ivy thatch. He seemed quite at home. He didn't budge when I got nearer. He sat and watched me as if to say, "Good evening, Annie, how are you?" He looked quite cozy, although he could easily have turned around and jumped down into the neighbor's garden on those strong back legs of his. Then he'd run off and not know where he was and get lost in the back gardens and be too scared to hear my call and then he'd scramble over the rear wall and into the street where for sure he'd run under the wheels of a car and get killed. I managed to smile at him, admiring how well he'd tucked himself among the thick, dusty leaves. He blinked his green eyes at me but didn't stir. I backed away and looked around for Lucille. She'd settled in her cracked ferns and seemed asleep.

9:13 p.m. Henry's still out on top of the wall. He's been there all evening. He seems to be enjoying himself immensely. Every so often I've gone out to visit him, gazing at his face up in the ivy while he watched me. He's stayed far away from Lucille and felt the breeze in his fur. It's dark now and I can only make out the shape of his plump little body. I called Andy an hour ago. She said he was making up his mind about whether to trade a life of luxury for the old freedom.

10:25 p.m. I went out into the garden about ten and walked over to him, even though the green ivy hid his face. Not wanting to turn the garden light on lest it scare him, I stood on tiptoe in the dark, peering in his direction while the crickets swelled. He still didn't stir. I began to think he had no intention of leaving, just liked sitting there. Nevertheless, in the old Catholic way, I lifted up my hand and gave him a blessing to keep him safe, just in case he decided to go. After a minute, I turned and slipped back inside, leaving the door open.

After doing the rest of the dishes, I switched off the kitchen light and wandered into the living room with a glass of French wine. While I rummaged for a book, Henry appeared at the door, walked casually across the rug with his tail in the air, and went into the kitchen for a bit of supper. I laughed out loud, sat down heavily on the sofa, and waited until he came back into the room, where he practically belched and then circled around several times, squinching his legs lower and lower onto the rug until he dropped down completely and curled himself up like a comma. He seemed quite satisfied with himself and his evening.

Needless to say, I went to bed happy.

eptember

Sunday, September 21

Henry and Lucille have kept their truce, but she's been spending a lot of time in a closet on the third floor. The very closet I made up when Henry first came to live with me. The one with my Phillies sweatshirt on the floor. She goes up there and sleeps long hours. But she has to take medicine for her hyperthyroidism. So every afternoon around 5:30 we have "tuna time," when I dance around my yellow kitchen singing, "Tuna time, tuna time, nummy luscious tuna time," to some silly tune I've made up. I grind her pill with a mortar and pestle, open the can of tuna, hold the top against the can to pour the juice into a shallow blue saucer, sprinkle the powdered medicine in, and stir it up. All this time, Lucille makes frantic figure eights between my feet. As if I could forget she was there. Then I sashay over and put the plate down next to her water bowl. I stand still as a stone, listening to her loud, happy slurps.

Cathy and Silver observed this routine late this afternoon when they came to take me on an excursion to the river. Silver tapped his feet on the tiles in the front hall, nosed under the green sofa, and sniffed all around the living room. Just as I put Lucille's tuna juice down for her on the linoleum floor where the cat bowls are, Silver scooted into the kitchen. She hissed at him and he looked surprised, as if he wondered why any creature would hiss at a dog as friendly as he. She went right back to slurping up her treat. When she'd finished, she stepped out into the living room and stopped on the chestnut floorboards, ignoring Silver who was poking around across the room near the garden doors, and started washing her face. I could have watched her for the full five minutes it would take her to primp, but Cathy was getting restless. She did a little jig, a kind of tap dance routine, starting on the Oriental rug and backing up for a final flourish where the rug ended on the floor. Then she swooped down and picked up Silver's leash. "Hi-ho, Silver! Go for a walk."

Following them out the door, I touched one of the tiny flecks of garnet that seam the half-stone façade of my house. It's something I do for luck now and then. My Irish realtor pointed out the shiny garnet speckles when I first bought the house, saying they showed how much the original owner cared about the place when he built it back in 1930. The very fact of those garnets pleases me somehow.

Soon we were gliding down Pine Street under scattered clouds in the late September sunshine. I must say, on the whole, I do like the neighborhood. All sorts of people live here—older people as well as young families, gay couples, and lots of single people. We passed houses of architects and professors and also met the two Carroll sisters, the middle-aged Irish-American ladies from Waverly Street, a block over, who were taking a walk. Their dad was a cop and they've lived in their house all their lives. The guy who owns a home across the street spent his childhood there in the 1930s and has never left. He told me that whole villages from Ireland came to work in the textile mills on the river in the nineteenth century.

We ambled two blocks west, past gingko trees with their lovely fan-shaped leaves. Silver trotted happily ahead, his claws making little tapping sounds on the brick pavement. Cathy and I had some desultory chat about my video—which, by the way, that canny sales manager Frank Lavelle and his boys have lapped up. I weaved around a stop sign, feeling the breeze ruffle my new layered hairdo. Then I said exactly what I thought. "The sales guys like nothing better than a video that tells the client all about the product—so they won't have to."

She grinned. "Yeah, yeah. Easy for them. They just pop the thing in the player and sit back."

"Bingo. Instant sales."

Cathy's done video in the past—lots of interesting museum installation stuff—and she knows a lot of the film crews in Philly. As we crossed into the Taney playground, we degenerated into speculation about whether or not my director—crazy and talented as he is—has a girlfriend or a boyfriend. Girlfriend, we decided.

At the community gardens, Cathy strode on ahead, her green ethnic dress billowing behind her. She and Alan "farm" a plot about twelve feet square, halfway down a short path in the center of the community allotments. There must be about sixty beds in all, full of beans and daylilies and sunflowers and such. Cathy reached down and broke off some stunning red zinnias she's grown. She has cherry tomatoes, too, which she pulled off by the handful and plopped into a plastic bag. "Basil's looking a little ratty," she said. "Neighbors will scoff." Not for the first time, I took against these community garden people. The folks who run the place are snooty. To even gain permission to work a plot, you have to get on a list kept by some woman in a Laura Ashley-type straw hat and, once you have a plot, you have to give it back after six years or some such thing. Can you imagine? Giving your bit of earth *back*? I'd feel like a tenant farmer. Didn't my ancestors leave Ireland for that very reason? Not to mention the fact that the community garden people compete like mad. They come around inspecting each other's crops and actually have prizes for the best tomatoes, etc. Cathy doesn't care a damn, of course. She does exactly what she pleases, and sometimes she remembers to water down here, and sometimes Alan does, and sometimes the basil just goes thirsty and grows scrawny and limp. Like now.

"Where's the river?" I said, ready for something wild and free and open, running unconstrained. She wrapped her plastic bag, spilling over with cherry tomatoes, around her wrist and picked up Silver's leash. Then she led me a few blocks over to the Walnut Street Bridge, an inelegant structure built by the highway department. Less than halfway across, an unmarked gap in the guardrail opened onto wide concrete steps. Keeping my eyes on my feet, I walked down the first flight of stairs, trailing behind Cathy and Silver who clattered merrily on. At the first curved landing, I looked up. There lay the cardboard-brown river. It seemed far away, at least two flights below me. A breeze brushed my face as I returned to my task. The soles of my shoes gripped each concrete step. On the ground, the aroma of a homeless guys' camp muddied the air. I slid through weeds and dirt until I reached the slippery bank. There at last the scent of water rose to meet me and blue-green waves coursed across the surface of the stream like scalloped scales. Unstoppable, the tidal river ran toward the sea. Exulting, I watched the current flow relentlessly downstream.

After a while, I turned and caught up with Cathy. She'd let Silver off his leash and he sprinted ahead while we walked along a rough path parallel to the water and the railroad tracks. She complimented my new hairdo. "Looks great. I like the way it frames that oval face of yours." Did she like the color, I asked? The reddish highlights on a brunette base? She did, of course. She's so sure of her own beauty that she can be generous to other women. Still I kind of rocked my head to and fro, very pleased with myself, as we wandered along. Weeds and wildflowers grew with lovely abandon at the edges of the path. After we'd meandered for ten minutes or so, I stopped for a moment, relishing the pollen and the vista of bridge after bridge. The late afternoon sunlight picked out yellow goldenrod and butterfly weed with its orange flowers. Cathy considered this extravaganza her very own florist shop, so we broke off huge stalks of Queen Anne's lace with its dusty white blossoms. I bent over to pull up blue cornflowers, practically by the roots, from the rocky soil near the tracks. We could have been in a wildflower meadow in deepest country. We weren't, of course. Freight trains groan along that stretch of CSX track night and day. Cars and trucks thunder on the expressway just on the other side of the river, but for today I didn't care. We walked on, clutching our bouquets, Cathy's sandals slapping the dirt. Every now and then, Silver circled back to see us and then rollicked on down the path, past dirty rolled-up blankets where, doubtless, homeless guys slept at night. We walked upstream for a while toward the Art Museum, but my eye kept catching spots of light on the tips of the waves, and I turned around to see the sun set gold and darting on the ceaseless river.

On the way home, I thanked Cathy profusely. Now I knew I could go down and walk along the river whenever the mood struck. I'd found that openness and ease which the natural world brings me, even in the city. "Glad to help," she said. She didn't think it was any big deal, but she did understand. "The wildflowers will look great in your big blue jug," she said. "They'll only last a day, but hey." She pulled four gangly cherry tomato stems out of her bag and shook them, scattering good Philly dirt on the pavement. "For your dinner."

"Just the ticket," I said and skipped in to see what was up with Henry and Lucille.

October

Monday, October 20

I've taken a few walks by the river myself recently, enjoying its power as I stride beside it. The river is a year-round thing, but it felt a little nippy down there yesterday. I've learned to listen for freight trains when I'm about a block away from the stairs on Walnut Street. CSX, which used to be the great Chesapeake and Ohio Railway, discourages people from going down near the river, which runs next to the tracks. Cathy says they park their biggest trains right there, just to annoy us. Oh never mind. If a freight idles, I stand on the bridge above and spot logos on the refrigerator cars until it moves on. Needless to say, my favorite is the sleeping cat silhouette on the older CSX cars, but I recognize lots of symbols—that's what comes of having a dad who worked in the railroad's legal department.

Henry and Lucille sat together by the fire last night in my living room. I'm loving the new high-gloss yellow paint on the walls in there. It positively sparkles in candlelight. For a while, both cats curled like bookends in front of the mesh fire screen. Then Henry got very playful. First he poked around behind the Indonesian linen wall hanging, becoming a moving bump behind its orange fringe. When he emerged from this lair, I slipped off my sofa and knelt on the floor, where I rolled walnuts and corks for him to chase. He scooted after a thick cork from a champagne bottle, leapt on it, and batted it around with his paws until it disappeared under the radiator, which clanged companionably. He got down on his haunches, then leaned on his right side, reached out his paw, and tried to angle the cork out. But it was stuck behind the dusty radiator pipe and he couldn't budge it. He got up and wandered aimlessly for a few feet. Then I rolled a walnut for him and he practically hopped across the rug, springing up with his back legs and coming down to a full stop on his front paws. He batted the walnut around like a hockey puck. All this while, Lucille sat in front of the crackling fire with her paws tucked under her. Manic activity is supposed to be one of the symptoms of hyperthyroidism, but she sure doesn't show it. Maybe she's getting better—or maybe she thinks she's too mature for all this cork-chasing nonsense. Anyway, it felt lovely to be there with them on a quiet Sunday evening. Leaning back on my butt while Henry hunted things, it occurred to me that the house sounds have become familiar. I'm used to the way the chestnut floors creak and the fridge hums in the kitchen. Picking myself up, I rooted around in a pile of shelter magazines—Cathy calls them decorator porn—on the coffee table. *Elle Décor* headlined "Fall Glamour." Just the ticket. I grabbed it and curled up on the sofa, tucking my legs under me, flaky with dry skin though they may be. All three members of my household felt quite content, absurdly cozy.

In bed a few hours later, I dreamed that Henry had died and I would have to write about it in this journal, but of course that's not one bit true. He's chock-full of life. Most days, he gallivants around, skitters walnuts, and has a fine time. He likes to play with the Phillies shoestring Andy sent home for him. First, he stretches out like a sphinx, points his ears forward, and lets me pull the string through his front legs. Then he holds it down with one firm paw until I let go. We can play this game for ten minutes at a stretch. He still doesn't let me pet him, but he smells my hands and feet. Now and then he'll leap onto the kitchen table, jut his nose out, and sniff me if I lean my face down toward him. It's as if he's investigating some brand-new territory.

December

Saturday, December 6

Guess what. Frank the chief sales manager actually came through with a prize for my video—a hard plastic pyramid that reads: *Achievement Award, Anne Kaier.* OK, nice enough. Very pleasing, in fact, for all that work, although I loved every minute of our shoot.

Better yet, the prize came with a fat check. So today Tommy and I went to New York to spend some of the money. I could have gone by myself, but it seemed like an excellent idea to bring Tommy along. He's clever and fun to be with; we like to hang out. I figured to be the groovy aunt and treat him to something unusual, a trip to the Big Apple. When I called to ask him if he'd like to go, he agreed right off the bat. Not shy about shopping, that boy. Our target stores were FAO Schwarz and Georg Jensen Silversmiths, in that order. Back when Tommy's parents got married in 1976, I went to New York to buy them a wedding present. I had my eye on a lovely silver candy dish—hand-hammered, if you please—made by those skillful Danes at Georg Jensen's. Pricey, for sure, but I reckoned Ed was my only sibling. I knew from the way he always admired Mom's wedding silver that he would like this little Jensen dish. But I also wondered when I'd ever get some silver of my own. So here's the deal. I'm fifty-two, I just got a prize for a piece of good work that I did myself. Time to bring my own slice of silver into my own house and use it to entertain my own friends.

First stop: FAO Schwarz. I figured it was best to get Tommy his gift right away so he wouldn't be too antsy when we got to Jensen's. He marched through Schwarz's huge doors on his long legs as if he owned the place, but he slowed down when we got inside. The sheer size—all those aisles and big windows, toy displays everywhere—kind of overwhelmed both of us. But Tommy soon hit his stride. He raced around for a while, checking everything out while I admired the clock in the middle of the store with its cheerful, old-fashioned doll face. Tommy fingered a stuffed monkey eating a banana, but then he moved on to something more fun: a rocket you can send up into the air.

With this rather alarming toy safely bagged, we cruised over to the Georg Jensen shop on Madison Avenue. Inside the velvety store, brilliant spotlights picked out glittering watches and silver candleholders. After looking around, Tommy and I scrunched up on high stools at the counter while a slender saleslady in a Hermès scarf bent from the waist to pull out a tray of serving spoons. Much to my delight, he sensed that this was a big deal for me and paid close attention. Six lovely spoons lay on the black velvet, each a graceful four inches of sterling silver. "Look, Tommy, you can see the little marks where the man's hammer fell when he made it."

"Cool."

Lifting up a spoon, I ran my thumb along the slender loop of silver which curved into a leaf at its handle. "Oh, how lovely," I murmured half to myself. This elegant, airy spoon would clearly please me. I looked at the sales-woman. "It's a Peapod pattern, yes?"

"Yes indeed." She had a slight European accent. "In-troduced in 1915." She smoothed the velvet.

"What do you think, Tommy?" I asked.

He hugged one of his knees and rocked a little. "You should have six of them, Annie." I laughed with delight. What a lovely thing to say. It seemed simple to him: I liked the spoons, and I should have all of them, for the pure joy of it.

I leaned down towards him as he tapped the nearest spoon, making it rock up and back. "Wish I could, Tommy." The spoon sparkled in the spotlight. "It's much too expensive for six, but we can definitely get one." The sales woman smiled her approval.

On the train ride home, with my elegant spoon in its maroon box safely tucked on the floor next to my feet, I kept thinking of Tommy's idea that I should have half a dozen. I loved the straightforward way he'd said it, his simple, almost factual notion that I was worth six spoons. What a lovely kid. It occurred to me that I simply liked him for himself, as a friend, that I was lucky to have such a charming, cool nephew—and that we should go to New York more often.

Back at my house, after we'd had a pizza and some ice cream, Tommy opened the garden door, blew into the air, and announced that he could see his breath. Then he started to hint around that he could probably figure out how to use the rocket as a firecracker and set it off on New Year's Eve. I confess I didn't want to hear about these calculations in great detail, and I sent him off to bed with a kiss and a pat on his blond crew cut. His parents can deal with the firecracker idea.

While I cleaned up the kitchen, Henry ambled in. He collected all four limbs together, sat up straight, and meowed. I stopped wiping the counters. "How's my boy?" He shook one of his paws and blinked his eyes at me. Leaning down, I held out my right palm. He stretched his neck about as far as it would go, smelled, and then rubbed my hand first with one side of his warm face, then with the other, scraping me gently with his whiskers. I think it's the first time he's touched me voluntarily. "You're putting your scent on me, Henry." I scratched him behind his ear and held half his face in my hand before he skittered away.

A memorable day.

Tuesday, December 16

Perhaps if I write about Lucille, thinking on paper,
I can figure out how to woo her again. Because I've lost
her—almost. She's about to sue Henry for alienation of my
affections. He's pushed her, my saucy Lucille, out of my
room, off her pillow, and out of my bed. She's never there
now, breathing softly, steadily, next to me. I can't wriggle
my nose in her neck fur and smell her laundry-fresh scent.
How can I coax her back?

Henry sat on my bed quilt and played with my hand
this morning. He caught my index finger in his teeth and
munched softly on it, but I jerked it away before he got
rough enough to break the skin. Then I got up and plucked
Lucille from the floor, hugged her, and sat with her in my
oak rocking chair, rubbing my cheek across her shoulder
as if to get my scent on her, so she'll remember me.

I will make more jottings. Looking back, it seems
wooing Henry was much easier than this new project of
reclaiming Miss Lucille. She used to chat with me every
day. I feel so lonesome without her.

ebruary

Thursday, February 19, 1998

Lucille died this morning. She died early this morning. God, I loved her and she loved me. She died in a corner of my bedroom. She was companionship and touch, warmth in my bed. She was endorphins! She was, for years, the only touch I had. And she was savvy and funny and sweet.

Her kidneys must have failed. For about a week before she died, she slept all the time on my Phillies sweatshirt in the third-floor closet, leaving her long white whiskers on the red fabric. I thought she'd found a cozy place where she could hide from Henry.

Last night, before bed, I went upstairs and lifted her out of the closet. She groaned once or twice, but I cushioned her against my terry-cloth bathrobe and brought her downstairs to my bedroom. I rocked her in my chair, worrying about what to do, not really wanting to face how sick she was. The fur behind her left ear still smelled sweet when I kissed her. "If you're not better by the morning," I told her, "I'll take you to the vet." Then I held her in my arms tight as tight and when I put her down she groaned again but made herself comfortable on the rug under my night table. In bed, I read for a while, trying to block out my fears, but I kept thinking her sickness didn't seem as terrible as it would have been if Henry hadn't come to live here. Before I turned out the light, I crept down, moved the lamp's electric cord away from her face, and patted her soft head.

Early this morning before I got out of bed, Henry had been wrestling with me. He'd walked up next to my itchy legs and flung himself against them. When I put my hand out, he'd sniffed it with his cool nose and then pounced on my arm, which I drew under the covers. Lucille must have heard all this. Was she angry? Too sick to care? I hate to think she felt I'd betrayed her. She must have died soon after Henry and I quieted down. When I climbed out of bed, I saw her silent body near my night table. I knew she was gone, though her back still felt warm.

After work, Andy and I buried Lucille in the pet graveyard behind Andy's house. I held my cat, stiff with rigor mortis, in my arms while Andy dug the grave with her spade. Lucille's hair still sprang lightly and the fur behind her left ear, which I have kissed a thousand times, kept its familiar brown. There in the rain, Andy scraped earth from the bottom of an oval hole. When she'd finished, I leaned down and laid Lucille in, tucking a blue towel around her. "Thank you, Lucille," I murmured, by which I meant to thank her for the ten years of company she gave me, for every saucy meow and every time she warmed my lap. After a minute, I stepped back while Andy shoveled in the dirt. Bit by bit the brown soil covered Lucille. We shaped the earth into a mound and arranged some stones around the top. Andy promised to plant a daffodil on the grave tomorrow.

Saturday, February 21

Like the sweet brother he is, Edward called today to say how sorry he was that Lucille had died. Then he added, "I hope Henry honors his part of the bargain and is ready to keep you company." Indeed he is. Right at this moment, he's sitting in the sunny place in the garden where Lucille used to sit. He sleeps on my bed. He meows and purrs and puts his soft, blond face right up to mine, twitching his whiskers.

But it's a whole new world with Henry—I'm not so possessive, though I finally got his collar on him, complete with my name etched in block letters. He can wander in and out whenever he wants, using his fine new cat door. He comes and goes and climbs up and down his yew tree and sits on the wall and then bounces into my living room. He's a sweet, loving creature—quite domesticated.

Truth to tell, I think Henry figured out that my house is a good home long before I did. That night when he sat on the garden wall and I feared he'd leave, he had no intention of going. He knew perfectly well that ours is a lovely place, rich with sunny spots to curl up in, occasional dishes of tuna fish juice, and someone who'll play around with walnuts on smooth chestnut floors. A place to stay, to settle. I just had to follow his lead. With Tommy visiting now and then, with friends to meet in the local bistro, and with Henry sidling up to my thigh when I'm on the sofa reading, I'm here, solid, home.

Epilogue

For about a year, Henry was my only cat. We lived in happy harmony. Then I began to tell Andy that maybe he would like a pal—someone to play with when I wasn't home. "He needs a kitten, a froufrou, some little piece of female fluff who will roll over on her back and say, 'Oh, Henry, you're so big and strong.'"

Andy looked at me over the rim of her glasses. "A little piece of female fluff, eh?"

About a month later, my friend Cathy told me about three kittens—all six weeks old. Their mother cat had nursed them and a musician had hand-raised them in Germantown with all the funky, artsy types who live there. Now they were weaned and ready for new homes. On a raw winter evening, I went over to the musician's house to pick one out. In a shed out back, two gray kittens and a tabby tumbled over their mother. In *Choosing the Right Kitten for You*, the author suggests you pick the kitty that comes up to you, for he or she will be the friendliest. But when I lifted up the tabby—reluctant as she was—and stroked her beautiful back and saw the stripes like a cancan dancer's stockings on her legs, I thought I had a froufrou for Henry.

Except that Hilda, as she came to be called, no more resembled a froufrou than Lucille had. Even as a kitten, Hilda made it quite clear that she was in charge. She had to have the best of everything: the best places to nap, the sunniest spots on the floor, the best bites of chicken. But she and Henry took to each other immediately. She followed him around everywhere when she could barely jump up one stair at a time. She snuggled next to him in the big wing chair during the winter, and when spring came she followed him out to the garden. He showed her how to climb the wall and visit the neighbors' fish pond. She grew and lengthened out—and became more and more beautiful and more and more fearless. Now, on summer nights, she chases fireflies and runs up the yew tree into the topmost branches.

Henry and I just sit below and watch.

Book club guide

Book lovers who like to lose themselves in a good memoir—or whose cats walk across their laps while they are reading—will enjoy *Home with Henry*. Consider reading it with your book club. Here are some questions to get your discussion started.

1. Anne kept the stray, feral cat that she picked up in the road. Why do you think she brought Henry home to live with her?

2. *Home with Henry* touches on many themes including identity, family, and living a rich life as a single woman. What other themes do you see in the memoir?

3. Anne's friends, Andy and Cathy, gave her moral support and practical tips, such as the idea of using her hand as a kind of paw to push food to Henry. What role do these friendships play in Anne's life? How do you see similar relationships enriching your own life, perhaps at particular times of need or transition?

4. Why do you think Henry hid under the bed for so long?

5. Anne's nephew Tommy plays a big part in the memoir. What about him makes the boy so important to

her? Talk about the ways in which your family members are similarly important to you.

6. Most women of Anne's generation, who grew up in the 1950s and early 1960s, expected to marry—and certainly expected to marry before they settled into a permanent home. How much do you think times have changed?

7. "When I rolled a walnut for Henry to chase, he practically hopped across the rug, springing up with his back legs and coming down to a full stop on his front paws. He batted the walnut around like a hockey puck." —October 20

   Anne clearly spent a lot of time observing her cats. What can you tell about Anne as a character from her interactions with them? If you have a cat or know a cat well, how might you describe him or her as a character?

8. How did you react to Lucille's death?

9. The memoir is structured as a diary—so Anne doesn't know what will happen next as the story unfolds. How does this structure affect your reading experience?

10. The book is full of images of closed and open doors, gated communities, and open places—such as the river. What do you think is the significance of these images?

11. "I went out into the garden about ten and walked over to him, even though the green ivy hid his face. Not wanting to turn the garden light on lest it scare him, I stood on tiptoe in the dark, peering in his direction while the crickets swelled. He still didn't stir. I began to think he had no intention of leaving, just liked sitting there. Nevertheless, in the old Catholic way, I lifted up my hand and gave him a blessing to keep him safe, just in case he decided to go. After a minute, I turned and slipped back inside, leaving the door open." –August 26

One of the climactic scenes takes place in the garden when Anne visits Henry, who is sitting on the wall. What do you think is really going on in this scene?

12. How did Anne's relationship with Henry help her to get used to living in her new home?

Acknowledgements

Many smart people have listened to my cat stories over the years and encouraged me as I wrote this book. I'd like to thank them.

Dr. Reginald L. Royster, Jr., D.V.M. and his staff at the Haverford Animal Hospital treated Henry with kindness and skill. Dr. Royster also read drafts of the book with an eye for veterinary accuracy.

Andy Brakman and writer Lynn Detweiler at Shared Medical Systems shored up my efforts to tame a feral cat.

My friends Joellen Brown and J.C. Todd gave me canny literary advice on early drafts.

Publisher Carla Spataro and editors MaryAnn Miller and Tara Smith at PS Books offered early faith and excellent editing. My friend ML Riley read the final draft with a red pencil and often gave me shelter in Maine.

Carol Chu's marvelous illustrations brought new life to Henry and Lucille. And Sarah Eldridge, my talented book designer, gave the book visual style.

My family was involved at every stage. My brother Ed has always been my stalwart support, my sister-in-law Netchen loves all animals, niece Liz Laffont encouraged me while I was taming Henry, nephews Charlie and Tommy Kaier directed a book trailer and Tommy read drafts and added spicy details, especially about firecrackers.

About the author

Anne Kaier's work has been published in venues such as *The Gettysburg Review, Alaska Quarterly Review, The Kenyon Review, Referential,* and *Beauty is a Verb: An Anthology of Poetry, Poetics, and Disability*, which is on the American Library Association Notable Books list for 2012. One of her essays appears on the list of "Notables" in *Best American Essays* (2014). *Malade*, a liter-ary memoir about disability, sexuality, and the Catholic shrine at Lourdes, is available from Shebooks.net. Holding a Ph.D. from Harvard University, she teaches creative writing and literature at Arcadia University and Rosemont College. Anne lives in Center City, Philadelphia.

Visit www.annekaier.com for free bonus features including the pamphlet *Tall Tails: How to Write about Your Cat.*

CPSIA information can be obtained at www.ICGtesting.com
Printed in the USA
BVOW06s2145090316

439790BV00014B/99/P